Contents

Introduction

Advertising has been an integral part of the media since Ancient Roman times. Advertising can persuade you to part with your money, save it, or give it away. It can persuade you to believe in certain values, or it can save your life. It has provided modern culture with an entire vocabulary of phrases and images, while at the same time it can induce suspicion, distrust and moral outrage.

Focusing on the UK advertising industry, this book examines these issues and deals in particular with how they affect our understanding of advertising's relationship with the media in which it appears.

The origins of advertising

Advertising is not a recent idea — in fact it is as old as the media in which it appears.

The earliest advertisments that we can identify have been discovered on the walls of excavated buildings in ancient Rome and Pompeii. These were painted directly onto the walls of the buildings and featured subjects that are familiar in advertisements today, such as houses available for rental. A particularly interesting example from Pompeii was an advertisement for a restaurant situated in another town. This was a very early example of advertising relating to travel.

In the Middle Ages, advertising was one of the functions of the town crier. By this time many people lived together in towns and villages but most were unable to read, so criers had the job of reading public notices aloud. However, they could also be paid by local business people to praise their products or services.

Printing and colonialism

Printed advertising did not become commonplace until the invention of the printing press with movable type, in the fifteenth century. This enabled advertisement material to be duplicated and reused. With the colonization of America, advertising became an important communications medium for information about products, particularly those that were important to the new settlers, such as medicines and agricultural goods. The lack of road and rail links meant that large-scale retailing had yet to develop. Printed advertising was the only efficient way of attracting customers, who would then have their goods delivered direct to their homes.

This advertising business

It might be said that advertising first developed as an industry in its own right in the European

'Dost thou seek reliefe from ye colde and flue symptomes?'

Advertising's influence on the news media is sometimes controversial today.

When town criers gave spoken advertisements along with their news, might they have been an early example of a controversial influence? If a crier announced an infectious illness in a nearby town, an enterprising dealer in medical remedies might well have paid the crier to praise the effectiveness of his wares!

A 19th-century town crier.

M E D I A   F O C U S

C

Advertising

Roger Thomas

Heinemann
LIBRARY

First published in Great Britain by Heinemann Library
Halley Court, Jordan Hill, Oxford OX2 8EJ
a division of Reed Educational and Professional Publishing Ltd.
Heinemann is a registered trademark of Reed Educational & Professional Publishing Ltd.

OXFORD MELBOURNE AUCKLAND
JOHANNESBURG BLANTYRE GABORONE
IBADAN PORTSMOUTH (NH) USA CHICAGO

Designed by Visual Image
Printed in Hong Kong

04 03 02 01 00
10 9 8 7 6 5 4 3 2 1

ISBN 0 431 08215 4

This title is also available in a hardback library edition (ISBN 0 431 08211 1)

British Library Cataloguing in Publication Data
Thomas, Roger
　　Advertising. – (Media focus)
　　1. Advertising – Juvenile literature
　　I. Title
　　659.1

Acknowledgements
The Publishers would like to thank the following for permission to reproduce photographs:
Advertising Archives, pp. 6, 20, 22, 26, 27; Audio Arts/David Troostwyk, p.28; Mary Evans Picture Library, pp. 4, 5; Forward Publishing, pp. 18, 19; Q Magazine/David Sheppard; p. 29; Robert Harding, p.13(bottom); Middlesex County Press Ltd, pp.16, 17; The Mirror, p. 14; Pan Books Ltd, p. 11; Penguin Books, p.10; Rex Features/Charles Ommaney, p.24; Frank Spooner Pictures, p.8; Tandy, p. 23; Tony Stone Images, p.13(top); Wycombe Swan Theatre & Town Hall, High Wycombe, p.9.

Commissioned photography by Chris Honeywell.

Cover photograph reproduced with permission of Tony Stone Images/Suzanne & Nick Geary.

Our thanks to Steve Beckingham, Head of Media Studies, Fakenham College, Norfolk for his comments in the preparation of this book.

Every effort has been made to contact copyright holders of any material reproduced in this book. Any omissions will be rectified in subsequent printings if notice is given to the Publisher.

Any words appearing in the text in bold, **like this**, are explained in the Glossary.

During the seventeenth and eighteenth centuries the first advertising agents conducted their business in the coffee-houses.

coffee-houses of the seventeenth and eighteenth centuries. Coffee was a novelty at the time and the coffee-houses were fashionable meeting-places where leading figures of political, literary and commercial life would gather to meet their friends and business associates.

Newspapers and journals had become very popular even by the mid-eighteenth century, which saw 11 million newspapers being sold in the UK every year. As this trend continued, some businessmen became aware that they could 'bulk-buy' large quantities of advertising space in these publications at a discount. They would then divide this up into smaller spaces and sell them on to other businessmen. Everyone gained from this arrangement. The publisher had a guaranteed income and the 'bulk-buyer' would make a profit on each space, while his customers were able to buy space according to their needs, with some of the discount being passed down to them.

These 'bulk-buyers' were the forerunners of today's advertising agencies. Today, however, most agencies can provide a wide range of facilities in addition to **media buying**, including research, design and production services. Ironically, however, the original idea of buying space with a view to re-selling it at a profit – known today as 'broking' – is generally not accepted in today's advertising industry! This is mainly because of the stringent controls that are in place, governing all aspects of the business. A publisher today would not agree to allowing anonymous advertisers to reserve space, as the advertiser may be in breach of the law or may want to place an advertisement that the publisher would not wish to have associated with their newspaper or magazine.

Advertising everywhere!

Today, advertising can be found in virtually any situation where information is being conveyed. Advertising media include the press, television, radio, posters and other outdoor media, packaging and the Internet. At the same time, advertising is now much more carefully controlled. Before legislation was passed which restricted the suggestions expressed in advertising, companies were able to make some extraordinary claims for their products. This persisted well into the 1950s and '60s. A memorable example was a TV commercial that showed a teenage girl who was unable to do her homework until she had taken a particular **brand** of laxative!

What advertising is

Advertising can be thought of in two ways:

One definition is that advertising is any form of public announcement that is designed to promote the sale of particular goods or services, or to persuade a group of people to carry out a particular course of action. This is certainly true in the sense that advertising is indeed supposed to do these things. However, there are many other ways of persuading people to want things, or to agree with your viewpoint.

For example, a clothing retailer may choose to buy advertising in a local paper to publicize their business. Alternatively, they may decide to sponsor a competition – e.g., 'Win a complete holiday wardrobe!' – and submit a professional photograph of the winner, decked out in their new clothes, to the newspaper, together with some **copy** about the business and the competition. This achieves a similar end – using the local paper to attract customers and paying for the privilege – but it is not really advertising. Why not?

A better, more practical definition of advertising is based on the idea that advertising can be bought, with a reasonable guarantee of the advertiser's message reaching the chosen audience. All other forms of publicity, including press and public relations, merchandising and so on, must also be paid for, but they do not buy an opportunity to reach a guaranteed and specified group of people with the exact message the advertiser wishes to communicate.

We all recognize this as being an advertisement. But how do we distinguish it from other kinds of publicity?

To use the example earlier, the newspaper may decide not to use the photograph and copy supplied by the clothing retailer, for any number of reasons, such as more urgent news items which needed to go in the space.

If the retailer chose to use an advertisement to publicize the shop, there would have been no potential obstruction to conveying the message. The retailer would have bought a precise opportunity to reach a group of potential customers, and would be able to specify:

• the size and position of the advertisement – e.g. a half-page in the holidays section of the paper
• the design and appearance of the advertisement – e.g. black and white, with a photograph included

Try raisin' the temperature.

Kellogg's Raisin Splitz
RAISIN IN THE MIDDLE

With hot milk on cold days.

When is an ad not an ad?

'Advertisements' for BBC publications and videos routinely appear on the BBC's supposedly advertising-free, license-funded TV channels. These caused complaints from the magazine industry, which claimed that this gave the BBC's publishing interests an unfair advantage. This is why 'plugs' for, say, the *Radio Times* on BBC TV include the words 'Other listings magazines are available' – in very small type!

• the message conveyed by the advertisement – e.g. 'Restock your holiday wardrobe on us!', with the implication that, if you don't win, you can buy the clothes from us anyway!
• the date the advertisement appears – e.g. during March, well after the January sales but well before the holiday season begins
• the audience for the advertisement – the newspaper having supplied an exact circulation figure, including the number of households within 'shopping distance' of the retailer.

So why try anything else?

Of course, what advertising does not convey is any kind of independent endorsement. Advertising is always understood to be an initiative on the part of the advertiser to persuade the public that a given product, service or course of action is desirable. Even when, for example, a washing machine manufacturer recommends a particular detergent, these recommendations are generally made in the context of a recognizable advertisement devised by both advertisers.

By contrast, a news item in a magazine devoted to a new product, or **product placement** in a film, or a **sponsorship** deal between, for example, a fizzy drink company and a music festival, conveys an additional positive image. The product is deemed to be newsworthy, or important enough to be associated with an event or art form that stands on its own merits and has no direct connection with the product itself. Companies usually aim to combine several of these techniques to promote their wares. This is known as the **marketing mix**.

New media, new dimensions

The Internet has added a new, interactive dimension to advertising, which is likely to be reflected in similar developments in the new field of **digital** television.

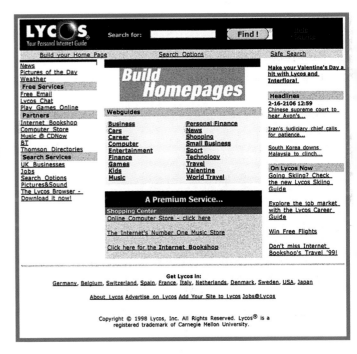

This Internet page from the Lycos browser also carries short 'prompts' from several advertisers. The advertisers can provide books, CD's and other products and services – even flowers! Clicking on the text provides access to these services. To compare this to conventional advertising, imagine if you could buy a product just by touching an advertisement for it!

What advertising is not

'Strictly speaking ...' – words you often hear when someone is trying to distinguish advertising from other forms of publicity!

However, if we consider advertising as the process of buying space or time in the media to reach a specified target audience, then there are several ways in which this can be done. Many companies often fail to consider these distinctions. People who work in marketing often say that the whole process of publicity is divided up in different ways depending on who is in charge of it. For example, someone trained in promotion management will tend to regard advertising and PR as parts of promotion, whereas someone trained in PR will regard advertising and promotion as offshoots of PR, and so on. Advertising is not...

that the right message will arrive in the right place. It can, however, cost a lot less! For example, the publishers of this book will have sent free copies to journalists working in the educational press, who may choose to write about it in magazines such as the *Times Educational Supplement*. If the book does receive **review** coverage, it will be an independent opinion, which carries a certain weight which advertising does not. PR budgets are often spent on a press reception and quasi-social events to which representatives of the media are invited, with a view to encouraging positive opinion in a relaxed atmosphere.

Press and public relations

This is best defined as the attempt to influence opinion via the media, by affecting the decisions made by: a) those who convey information in those media, and b) people who receive information from those media. In the case of large companies, staff are sometimes employed to deal directly with the opinion-forming public by answering queries, providing information, etc.

Public relations (or PR) is often expertly managed and can be very influential. However, it relies on journalists and other independent providers of news and formers-of-opinion to convey the message the company hopes to send. Unlike advertising, it does not guarantee

Sales promotion

This can take many forms, but it usually involves some sort of there-and-then direct access to the product. For example, discounts, free **samples** of cheese in a supermarket, a test drive of a new car or a sample of a beauty product on the front of a magazine are all sales

This is not an advertisement. (It's merchandising)

promotion ideas. However, any of these can be part of an overall **marketing campaign** which may include supporting advertising ('Test-drive one at your local dealer today!') and just having a brand mentioned will help to remind people of the product.

Merchandising

This consists of products such as T-shirts, posters and other consumer goods that are deliberately linked to another, often quite different, product or service, usually through the display of brand logos or other identifiable images. These are generally sold to the public and/or distributed free of charge within the client company's profession. For example, Roland, who manufacture keyboard instruments, produce items of clothing which their staff wear at exhibitions etc. and which are also on sale to the public. As these items are mainly bought by users of their music products, they encourage **brand loyalty** and a benevolent **cult following**.

Companies in the children's film and TV industries, such as Disney, are highly dependent on successful merchandising. However, these are products, not bought media, and while they can be extremely effective both as promotional items and as **profit centres** in their own right, they do not offer the same guaranteed message delivery as advertising. For example, a reader chooses to buy a film magazine for its editorial content – the advertising, for, say, the new Disney movie comes along with it. Buying a Disney lunchbox relating to the movie is, as it were, buying 'further into' another, already existing, product – the movie itself. Interestingly, in the case of high-cost original products, the merchandising

Corporate Hospitality

Full facilities are available for private receptions before, during the interval or after a performance. Many local companies and organisations have enjoyed the opportunity to entertain their staff and clients with a stylish reception and the best seats for a show. Many performances are also available for sponsorship.

Call 01494 514444 for further details.

Nor is this. (It's promotion.)

may be seen by the buyer as a token substitute for the product itself. Compare, for example, the number of Harley-Davidson T-shirts around to the number of Harley-Davidson motorcycles!

Sponsorship

This is where a company provides funds and/or support-in-kind to assist with another venture, often in the fields of the arts, entertainment or sport. The sponsor is usually associated with the event or venture to cultivate good public opinion. This is a frequently controversial area – for example, where tobacco companies sponsor sporting events. A sponsorship package directly underwrites some of the costs of the sponsored event, and may also include **corporate entertainment** opportunities, discounts on tickets, merchandising and so on.

All these and many other methods of publicity can be combined into a company's promotional strategy or **marketing mix**. While they are all related to advertising, they each differ in specific ways.

Is advertising good for you?

The very existence of advertising has always been controversial.

What is advertising *for?*

This is an important question in two senses. It is important to understand how advertising fits in with other forms of marketing and publicity, but it is also important to understand advertising's role in the media and in society in general.

One of the most informative books about the principles of advertising was written by David Ogilvy, who founded the Ogilvy & Mather advertising agency in the USA in 1949. Today, 'O&M' is an international company and is one of the top ten advertising agencies. An agency's performance is measured by its billings – i.e. the total amount of money that it receives from its clients for services provided and advertising bought on the clients' behalf.

Ogilvy on Advertising *was written by the founder of the ad agency Ogilvy & Mather.*

O&M currently bills just under £300 million per year in the UK alone.

David Ogilvy makes some interesting observations, both practical and moral, about what advertising actually does. The very first sentence reads: 'I do not regard advertising as entertainment or an art form, but as a medium of information.' This is an important point and was one of the first principles of even the very earliest examples of advertising.

The moral debate

The moral acceptability of advertising is sometimes questioned by people who believe that it is wrong to try to persuade people to part with their money. Ogilvy counters this by saying that people who have money generally enjoy spending it and are entitled to do so ('buying things can be one of life's more innocent pleasures'). This also includes making choices between ways of meeting essential needs – we all need to buy bread, but what sort and which brand do we choose? In other words, advertising is a way of persuading people to finalize their choices of how to spend their money.

This viewpoint contrasts interestingly with that of the American social critic Vance Packard, who published an equally well-known book in 1957 called *The Hidden Persuaders*.

Packard essentially believed that advertising was an evil attempt by big business to control the thinking of consumers. At the time, American manufacturers, particularly in the motor car industry, had just started to research the demand for products before they were launched, rather than learning from the success or failure of earlier products – a process that was very costly if a product proved unpopular. However, as market research had not yet become an established profession, manufacturers turned to psychologists for help, who of course described their findings in their own professional terms.

In his books on the marketing of arts events, the consultant, lecturer and author Keith Diggle questions the underlying assumptions made by Packard. Packard believed that advertising had become an all-powerful force and that its power to influence and control thinking was dangerous and evil. Diggle argues that advertising is simply one of the many forms of persuasion we encounter in daily life and, more importantly, disagrees with Packard's view that it is inherently wrong to try to persuade someone to want something they do not want already. He reasons, as did David Ogilvy, that people like wanting things. What do you think?

This influential book questions the moral acceptability of advertising.

Who?!

Four apparent traditions among advertising agencies:

1 they are often named after their directors

2 for some reason those directors often have unusual surnames (a fact enshrined in the satirical magazine *Private Eye* in the form of the fictitious agency Bogleby, Bargle and Pratt)

3 agencies often merge

4 the new group of directors – all of whom will have their own reputations and previous experience to bring to the new, merged organization – often have their individual identities preserved in the new company name.

This can lead to some extraordinary tongue-twisters, occasionally relieved by the use of initials. When the two agencies BMP and DDB merged, they wisely referred to themselves as BMP DDB rather than Boase Massimi Pollitt Doyle Dane Bernbach. However, one agency managed to turn this phenomenon into humorous **copy** for one of their own recruitment advertisements. Advertising for a receptionist/switchboard operator, they asked for the usual qualifications and experience, together with a willingness to repeat the agency's name when answering the phone hundreds of times a day. The agency – which, as it happens, never used its initials – was called Still Price Court Twivy D'Souza.

Which media?

Consumer choices are one thing – media choices are another. Or are they?

Custard for 250,000

In the planning stages of a large-scale advertising campaign, the advertiser – or the agency working on their behalf – needs answers to the following questions.

1 What is this product and who is it for? This will have been researched in advance and an effective way of conveying a message about the product will have been devised by a **creative team**.

2 How many of the right kind of people will the advertising reach (i.e. will have their attention drawn to the product) and at what cost?

The distinction between the purchasable commodity of 'advertising media' as described by the profession, and 'the media' (i.e. the mixture of information transmission systems in general use) as perceived by the public, is important here. The **media planner** looks at the range of available media and decides which will be the most appropriate. In the case of a new brand of instant custard, for example, the **media buyer** may reach these conclusions:

• TV advertising. *For*: obviously strongly visual, can be bought region-by-region if the product is to be **trialed** first. *Against*: can prove expensive when the **airtime** costs are added to the cost of producing the commercial. Tetley, the tea-bag manufacturers, recently tried a different approach to this. They distributed samples of a redesigned tea bag on a house-to-house basis, together with a brochure that not only asked for the householders' views on the new design but also provided **storyboards** for several possible TV commercials, asking for the householders' views on these, too. This was

Know your ABC1C2DE!

Most advertising relies on **demographics** – the measurement of the population in terms of occupation, age, gender and location. The traditional demographic categories are as follows:

A – Upper middle class, in upper managerial, administrative or professional careers.

B – Middle class, in intermediate managerial, administrative or professional careers.

C1 – Lower middle class, in supervisory, clerical, or junior managerial, administrative or professional jobs.

C2 – Skilled working class. Skilled manual workers.

D – Working class. Unskilled manual workers.

E – Lowest subsistence levels. State pensioners or widows (no other earnings), casual workers.

Until recently, these rather unflattering categories were central to choosing which media to use. For example, the *Sun* newspaper would be a likely medium for reaching a C1/C2/D/E readership. However, changing patterns of earning, spending and family structure, which became particularly noticeable during the 1980s, are not reflected in this approach. For example, a divorced and remarried B

TV advertising is widely used when targeting family audiences.

an interesting example of a sales promotion being used to refine the content of subsequent advertising.

• Radio advertising. *For*: can also be bought region-by-region and can be relatively

or C1 parent may be supporting two families, thus having less **disposable income** than these categories might imply. Also, the importance of brands cannot be reflected in this approach. For example, it can be shown that a group of A, B and C1 consumers would be more likely to buy larger, more luxurious cars than a C2/D/E group, but not whether they would choose a BMW or a Saab.

In an attempt to compensate for this, **demographers** have added a further level of classification, allowing for single-person households, one-parent families and so on. They now also take a person's lifestyle changes into account – for example, when someone is saving for a deposit on a house or becomes a parent.

inexpensive compared to TV airtime. Production costs, being sound-only, are low. *Against*: a loving verbal description of custard, unsupported by evocative visuals, is unlikely to sound convincing!

• National and/or regional newspaper advertising. *For*: can achieve very wide coverage of a suitable demographic group. *Against*: can be expensive and result in high **wastage**. (One way of getting round this is by advertising jointly with a regional retailer.) Also, the **production values** and **environment** offered by newspapers are not always compatible with a 'cosy' product such as a dessert food.

• Magazine advertising. *For*: advertising can be precisely targeted at likely buyers – for example, by using women's or home interest titles with large readerships. Production values, including quality colour printing and the advertising environment are likely to be good. *Against*: the product may need to be advertised in several magazines in order to reach a large enough target market.

• Outdoor advertising, such as posters or buses. *For*: high visibility, but … *Against*: often for very short periods of time. Complex messages are hard to get across with these media.

Why not advertise custard here?

The national press

Newspaper advertising is dependent on circulation, which is dependent on reader loyalty, which in turn demands that readers can relate to their newspaper.

Newspapers have been traditionally distinguished from magazines and journals because of the role they have in presenting information across a range of news subjects to a readership that accepts the way in which this information is presented. This notion of acceptance is extremely important – above all, readers should regard their newspaper as being 'on their side'. In the UK, the traditional distinction between newspapers has been between 'broadsheets' – the larger-format papers such as *The Times* and the *Daily Telegraph* – and the smaller-format 'tabloids' such as the *Daily Mail* and the *Sun*. The smaller format is said to have been devised initially for the benefit of commuters who read their newspaper on the way to work in the morning.

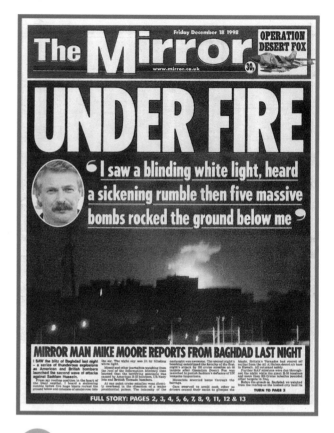

The *Mirror* *is the second most popular tabloid in the UK.*

Readership

Sixty-six per cent of the British public regularly read at least one of the national daily newspapers, which between them carry £1.5 billion worth of advertising each year. Of these papers, the *Sun* has the largest circulation (around 4 million copies per day) and the *Independent* has the smallest (just under 280,000).

Traditionally, the daily broadsheet newspapers are regarded as being more 'serious', catering for an educated, professional readership and carrying a higher proportion of **hard news** stories together with commentary on the news from informed specialists. The tabloids tend to give more emphasis to sensational, but not necessarily important, stories – particularly if they involve famous personalities. A useful way of monitoring this – which is also an interesting example of cross-media commentary – is to watch the BBC 2 TV programme *Newsnight*, which usually closes with a brief summary of the following day's newspaper headlines.

News + paper = newspaper?

One of the most important aspects of advertising in the national press is the realization that the diverse readerships available to advertisers have entirely different priorities. For example, *The Times*, whose readers are mainly in the A/B/C1 category, regularly carries advertising offering investment opportunities of a kind that would not appear in the predominantly C1/C2/D/E *Sun*. The latter, however, carries an alarming amount of advertising from companies offering loans. While this affects some people's opinions of these media, the reality is rather more interesting.

Despite their being lumped together as 'newspapers', the readerships of the broadsheets and the tabloids buy their chosen paper for subtly different reasons. For many tabloid readers, the primary source of hard news is television, rather than newspapers. This means that tabloid newspapers have traditionally contained more feature-based material: 'Ten top tips for a hassle-free holiday', or 'How to keep your partner from straying', for example. This has often been extended to regular features such as problem pages, horoscopes and medical advice columns, none of which have much to do with news.

This clearly has implications for the kinds of advertising that will sit comfortably in one type of newspaper or the other. For example, in addition to taking demographic considerations into account, a furniture chain may advertise on a large scale in certain tabloid newspapers in the knowledge that the paper will probably not contain a two-page feature on the problems of deforestation. Conversely, there

would be little point in Esso running corporate, opinion-forming advertising in a tabloid **environment** that contained little appropriate hard news encouraging this kind of thinking.

News from elsewhere

Of course, the spread of news media available to all demographic groups is now very large, encompassing the press, broadcasting (including **teletext** services), **online** services and even **rolling displays** in public places. This has meant that newspapers of all kinds are now becoming more like feature-led magazines, with a consequent effect on the range of advertising they carry. The Saturday *Guardian* is a good example.

This consumer advertising is far more likely to appear in the tabloids than in the broadsheets. Why?

The regional press

The notion of the relative power of 'regional' versus 'national' newspapers can produce guesses about circulation figures that are very wide of the mark.

The quiet giant

Regional newspapers in the UK are a very powerful force in the world of advertising. There are around 100 regional dailies and 1300 regional weeklies. In terms of advertising revenue (more than £2 billion per year, or 20% of the overall expenditure on advertising) the medium is second only to television. Research by the Newspaper Society – an organization representing the industry's interests – shows that 88% of all UK adults read a local paper and that 40% prefer their local paper to the national press. So regional newspapers represent an extremely valuable readership.

Not such small fry!

Surely a national newspaper is bound to sell more copies than one published for one particular area of the country only? In fact, this is often not the case. For example, in 1996 the Scottish *Daily Record* sold an average of 729,391 copies per day – more than the circulation of the *Guardian* (398,057) and the *Financial Times* (301,961) put together. Of course, Scotland is a nation and is only considered as a 'region' within the UK in marketing terms, so perhaps this is not entirely surprising. However, the penetration of even highly localized papers is extremely high. For example, the *Isle of Wight Sunday Press* sells around 40,000 copies – equal to one copy for every three residents of the island – and as local papers tend to be read by more than one person in a household, its overall readership is higher still.

To pay or not to pay?

The main distinction among regional (serving a fairly wide area) and local (often serving one town or locality) papers is between those that are bought by the readers and those that are delivered free of charge to all households within a specified area.

Free newspapers are weekly and their only source of revenue is advertising. They are obliged to attract a large volume of advertising in order to pay their entire running costs.

A typical local newspaper, offering detailed coverage of community issues.

They achieve this by producing very high **print runs**. For example, the *Manchester Metro News* has a circulation of over 300,000 – more than the national *Independent* – which, together with its free door-to-door distribution, means that it delivers a very high readership for advertisers. This distribution is then independently **audited** under a system called VFD, which stands for 'verified free distribution'. This ensures that the publisher's claims for the paper's circulation are accurate.

The equivalent procedure for 'paid-fors', as they are known, is run by the Audit Bureau of Circulations (known as the ABC – but don't confuse this with the demographic categories described earlier!). The local and regional 'paid-fors' compete directly for advertising with the free papers.

The arguments used by both sides when competing for advertising revenue are important indicators about how these two closely related media differ. Publishers of free newspapers can guarantee that a certain quantity of papers will be delivered to potential customers, but they cannot guarantee that all of these recipients read the paper, let alone read it in sufficient detail to receive the desired message from one particular advertiser. This problem can be offset to an extent by research which asks local residents which paper they read, but this will be based on a sample of the local population which is likely to be far less than the paper's VFD figure. For example, it would be impossible to ask all 201,328 readers of *The Glaswegian* whether they read the paper before discarding it.

Publishers of 'paid-fors' capitalize on this by drawing attention to the fact that, while their circulation figures are often smaller, their newspapers are specifically selected for purchase by the reader, the implication being that advertising in 'paid-fors' receives higher-quality attention than advertising in free

This regional press advertisement is of particular interest to local inhabitants.

newspapers. They will also argue that free newspapers offer a much poorer **environment** in terms of editorial/advertising ratio. As free newspapers are obliged to carry large volumes of paid advertising to cover their costs, the benefit to each individual advertiser is diminished. Not only is their advertising likely to be surrounded by that of competing organizations, but the sheer volume of advertising overall reduces the impact of any individual advertisement, making it harder to find and less likely to hold the reader's attention.

What kind of advertising?

Above all, advertising in the regional press is intended for a regional readership, even if it is part of a national campaign.

Magazines

As advertising media, magazines are proving surprisingly durable.

Who reads magazines?

Many people read magazines regularly; most people read them at some time or another. In editorial terms, magazines either tend to cover specialist subjects (anything from *BBC Gardeners' World* to *Dairy Farmer*) or take the lifestyle of their readers as a starting point and effectively build a magazine around it (e.g. women's magazines like *Woman's Realm*, or 'style press' magazines like *FACE*).

Magazine publishing maintains a traditional distinction between consumer magazines, which are bought by members of the public in support of their areas of interest, and trade magazines, which are about particular trades or professions and provide news and comment for people who work in them. There is a further subdivision in the trade press, as certain titles are distributed wholly or partly on a 'controlled circulation' basis. This means that they are sent free of charge to executives working in a particular profession. This is not an act of charity, but a means of attracting advertisers which is similar to that used by free regional newspapers, by guaranteeing that the publication will reach the right readership. As with newspapers, magazine circulations are monitored by the Audit Bureau of Circulations.

Given the enormous variety of magazines that exists, there are few potential markets for products and services that cannot be reached through the medium.

Magazines can be produced for very specific target markets, such as this one for Tesco shoppers who are interested in cooking.

The many-headed reader

In the case of consumer magazines, readers often strongly identify with the way in which a magazine presents itself and the kind of content that appears in it, even if the magazine serves only one of their interests. This is an important consideration for advertisers. For example, research has shown that the readers of *Hi-Fi Choice* magazine are enthusiastic hi-fi buyers, but they also tend to read the male lifestyle magazines such as *GQ*, and buy clothes. Yet the chances of advertising for clothing appearing in *Hi-Fi Choice* are slight. Why should this be?

The reason is that most consumer magazines present a self-contained worldview and assume that the reader has chosen a particular title for its content. An advertisement that is unrelated to this content can simply be a source of irritation. That said, when the *Hi-Fi Choice* reader picks up a copy of *GQ*, they effectively become a different reader with different expectations of what this different magazine will provide, making them receptive to entirely different advertising messages. While most consumer magazines are dependent on advertising, both **media owners** and advertisers are always mindful of this tendency.

While trade magazines are less dependent on this, professional readers always express preferences for some trade titles over others, so the process still applies. Many specialist consumer magazines are also influential in the trade sector, which affects the advertising they contain. For example, a CD advertised in *Select* magazine both encourages dealers to stock it and encourages consumers to buy it.

Anywhere and everywhere

Because of the ease with which magazines can be produced in comparison with, for example, a TV programme and the advertising that appears during the breaks, the medium is both internally adaptable – allowing for special **reader offers**, **advertorials** and **editorial sponsorship** – and can be slotted into many points in the chain of general production, marketing and consumption. For example, many supermarkets produce home interest magazines which are sold at checkouts. Free magazines are available to travellers on rail, sea and by air. New house-buyers can even be presented with a complimentary magazine

about moving house by their solicitor! In each case, precisely targeted advertising forms a part of the publication.

One of the most intriguing things about the present-day range of media available is the way in which any new development in media, communications or marketing immediately gives rise to new magazines relating to it as well as coverage in existing magazines, which could be said (often at a considerable push) to relate to the subject already. For example, all computer technologies in current use have magazines relating to them – *PC Format*, *Mac User* and so on – even obsolete computers that still have users have magazines about them. There are even magazines about mobile phones. Most interestingly, the medium that was supposed to do more to displace the printed word than any other – the Internet – supports a whole range of printed magazines!

The advertising in the Tesco Recipes *magazine is precisely geared to the readership.*

Global advertising

Global media means global advertising, and global advertising means global brand names and advertising campaigns that are recognizable throughout the world.

Why advertise globally?

Advertising, like all media phenomena, is tied to economic expansion. Wherever there are people, there are needs and desires; wherever there are needs and desires, there are markets for products and services; wherever there are markets for products and services, there is advertising. Also, the world's population is increasingly mobile. If an American tourist can see goods and services advertised in London that he or she might buy either in the UK or back home, then the advertising is clearly more effective. In any event, global economic expansion tends to make goods and services available worldwide.

There are, however, occasional problems. For example, the launch of a chocolate bar called 'Marathon' in the UK promoted a brand image associated with energy and sustenance. When this was changed to the fairly meaningless 'Snickers', to match the American brand name for the same product, many UK consumers thought the 'new' name was rather silly. Fortunately, the popularity of the product itself compensated for this.

The early history of advertising as an independent, functioning business took place mainly in national and regional markets which were still in a state of expansion and interconnection. For example, the progressive colonization of the USA, beginning at the turn of the seventeenth century, allowed the development of advertising across a territory that was expanding both literally and economically.

Global Advertising: this brand is available worldwide and can be advertised virtually anywhere.

However, the inevitable result of economic expansion is market saturation. This means that, theoretically, everyone who wants a product or service has bought it. In reality, of course, this never really happens. However, there may come a point when, say, 90% of those people in a given area who are likely to buy a particular brand and model of car have done so, and to persuade the remaining 10% to do so would require a marketing effort that would not be worth the investment.

There are then two strategies open to advertisers. They can advertise new products to replace the ones their customers have bought so far, or they can look to expand the market territory for their products.

Expanding the market

In fact, most companies mix both strategies, and the car industry provides many examples of both. For instance, the long-serving Ford Escort finally saturated its target market in 1998, and a new model call the Focus was advertised to the target market for whom the Escort was originally created. This strategy was aimed at encouraging the ownership of the new model among Escort drivers, but provided a fresh opportunity to attract buyers of broadly similar cars made by competing manufacturers.

Nevertheless, as Paul Simon's song had it, 'cars are cars, all over the world', and there has been a long history of progressive global branding in the car industry. However, had advertising for the following brands, all of which are now commonplace in the

UK, been seen in the UK media 30 years ago, the car-buying public would probably have had the following preconceptions about these exotic foreign brands:

- Volvo: obscure, sporty-looking thing driven by 'The Saint' in the TV series.
- Citroën: used by French police and farmers.
- Volkswagen: peculiar-shaped German toy invented by Hitler.
- BMW: the motorcycle you bought if you couldn't afford a Harley-Davidson.
- Toyota: posh Japanese sports car driven by James Bond in that one set in Japan!

The expansion of the markets for these brands has necessitated global advertising strategies, dependent on global media.

Media and markets worldwide

Many newspapers and magazines are published in several countries, such as the *International Herald Tribune* and *The Economist*. Many more are exported from their source country into foreign markets, and more still have counterparts serving the same kinds of readership in their home territory. Advertising for products and services that are available internationally are very much a part of this process.

An interesting exercise is to buy one or more imported consumer magazines from the USA or Europe (they are often available in independent newsagents in the UK) and make a list of the advertised brands that are available in the UK. Cars, drinks, perfumes, clothes, music products and even food products are often marketed and advertised in this way.

Global media: unusually, this French art magazine, which has English-speaking subscribers outside France, mixes French and English text in a single edition. One of its major advertisers is Jaguar – a global car brand of UK origin.

Television and radio

Television advertising is what comes to most people's minds whenever advertising in general is mentioned.

Despite the fees that advertising agencies charge for producing high-quality, memorable advertising for television, the pervading power of the medium is at least partly at the root of this. In the UK, 97% of households have a TV set, 64% have two sets, 28% have three or more, and 37% of households with children under 16 have TVs in the children's bedrooms. Forty per cent of the UK population's overall leisure time is spent watching TV. It is hardly surprising, therefore, that TV advertising is carefully regulated by the ITC (the Independent Television Commission).

Terrestrial commercial television – broadcast from land-based transmitters rather than by satellite or cable – comprises 16 regional 'channel three' stations, such as Carlton, HTV and Tyne Tees. The other non-BBC stations are Channel 4 (S4C in Wales) and the more recently launched Channel 5. Between them they attract £1.7 billion worth of advertising per year.

Satellite and cable TV

These alternatives to terrestrial television also carry advertising, but their **penetration** of the overall UK television audience remains quite small. For example, according to figures published for Spring 1997, 33.1% of all TV 'viewer-hours' are spent watching an ITV channel, whereas only 4.3% are spent watching any of the numerous channels provided by BSkyB, which dominates satellite TV in the UK.

The newest development in this field was the launch of digital television, providing many more channels of TV broadcasting. While this may theoretically affect the existing **market shares** for TV advertising, it is unlikely to affect the lead position occupied by independent terrestrial television in the immediate future.

Radiohead!

Radio advertising was first presented to a bemused British public by Radio Luxembourg in the 1950s. Since then, the rise of the commercial radio sector, both national (such as Classic FM) and regional (such as Capital) has provided an advertising medium that is particularly effective for

TV advertising like this is often spontaneously recalled.

Radio advertising can often work when visual advertising cannot.

Imaginary advertising

Several generations grew up with a vague distrust of television which, when added to the general distrust of advertising fuelled by the likes of Vance Packard (see pages 10-11), produced some amusing results. For example, in 1957 a market researcher named James Vicary theorized that advertising could be flashed so quickly onto a TV screen in the middle of a programme that viewers would be unaware that they had seen it. However, they would subconsciously feel the urge to buy the advertised product without being aware that they had been subjected to the advertising process.

regional and local advertising. The (sound only) production costs and **airtime** rates are considerably less expensive than for regional ITV, for example.

Radio is one of the few media that can transmit advertising information while the recipient is to all intents and purposes fully engaged in some other activity. For instance:

• Car radio. 'Drive time' – either of the two periods of the day when drivers are travelling to and from work – is an airtime slot that is highly sought-after by advertisers. Their near-captive listeners may not listen to the radio at any other time but many drivers tune in then because they rely on the radio for traffic reports.
• Radio in the home. Radio provides a popular background to housework and other domestic tasks.
• Radio in the workplace. This can range from a portable radio playing in the background of, for example, a garage, to **piped** radio in factories.

Although average listening figures have fallen slightly, they are unlikely to diminish significantly in the near future, simply because there is no obvious substitute for sound-only broadcasting. Indeed, the recent advent of digital radio, offering improved sound and more choice, may well increase overall listening.

This idea, known as 'subliminal' advertising, was used as a fictional device years later in the UK's *Max Headroom* TV show. In the story, these 'blipverts', as they were called, had the side effect of making the viewer explode! Not much opportunity for a **tracking study** there, then!

However, the reality is funnier still. The UK Institute of Practitioners in Advertising – a professional association of companies involved in the business – was very worried by the damage this idea could do to the image of advertising. The result was that the IPA issued an official ban on subliminal advertising, despite the fact that it did not exist.

The subject resurfaced in 1998, when an American padlock manufacturer claimed a large increase in sales after using a series of one-second TV commercials. However, one second is really too long for a truly subliminal effect – ordinary cinema film presents 24 images per second – so the campaign may well have succeeded because of its so called 'teaser effect'.

Outdoor and other media

Over the years, the concept of 'outdoor' advertising has effectively come to include any form of advertising that isn't obviously anything else.

A matter of definition

Advertising agencies that specialize in posters are more likely to diversify into other forms of non-press and non-broadcast media than to attempt to move into the buying of space and **airtime**. Broadly speaking, everything from poster hoardings to advertisements for breakfast cereals on milk bottles falls into this area. Cinema advertising is, however, an exception; it is a specialist area in itself.

The great outdoors ...

Posters were among the earliest forms of advertising and their sophistication has increased over the centuries.

In **creative** terms, there are really only two kinds of posters: **copy**-heavy and copy-light.

Posters that carry a large volume of text and/or complex illustrations are primarily designed to be read. Typical locations for

these are railway and underground stations, bus stops, waiting rooms and so on – in fact anywhere where the public's attention is likely to be available for the amount of time necessary to digest the content of the poster reasonably thoroughly. Typical subjects for such posters include:

• narrative advertising, such as a detailed description of how a drink is made
• a puzzle or word game to solve
• informative advertising, such as a poster for a concert series.

Of course, such advertising works in two ways. The reader may well see the poster on several occasions other than when the details are read. This can offer either a repeated invitation to study the poster in more detail or, if the reader has already done this, a reminder of the information it contains.

Posters such as these are widely used in advertising.

Posters that have very little copy are generally placed on sites where the public's attention is likely to be more cursory, such as a hoarding by the side of a busy road. Under these circumstances only a brief textual message can be conveyed effectively – sometimes no more than one or two words. Advertising of this kind often dispenses with text altogether, relying on just a visual image and possibly a brand name or logo.

The apparent simplicity of the poster has produced some sophisticated variations. The illuminated displays in Piccadilly Circus in London are a dramatic variation on the concept of the poster. Others in more widespread use include:

• illuminated poster sites at bus stops
• motorized 'rotating' posters which allow several advertisers to share the same site
• projected images which work in a similar way.

Occasionally, poster sites are exploited in very imaginative ways, such as the memorable instance of a real car being apparently 'stuck' onto a poster hoarding to advertise a super-strong glue.

... and elsewhere

As you will have seen from the above examples, poster advertising does tend to link naturally into other forms of non-press media. Known collectively as 'avant-garde' advertising, the media involved can be very diverse. For example, advertising:

• on theatre tickets
• in (and on) taxi cabs
• on food packages for related products – advertisements have been printed directly onto eggs!

Fly-posting

'Fly-posting' – displaying posters on illegal sites, such as disused shops – is possibly the greyest of grey areas in advertising.

Despite its 'underground' nature, an advertiser can often benefit from fly-posting. The music industry is one of several that gain from this form of advertising. The next time you see a cluster of posters for some new records plastered over a shopfront or fence, take a few minutes to check the information they carry. You'll see the artist's name, the title and possibly the artwork from their new CD cover, maybe even some tour dates. What you won't see is the name or logo of the record company or promoter. Clearly, they had nothing to do with these illegal posters, which were perhaps put up by hundreds of fans in the middle of the night. Funny, that …

Advertising gets everywhere – even on car park tickets.

Attitudes to advertising

Advertising provokes controversy.

The ongoing debate

There remains a vague belief that advertising should not exist at all, as it encourages unnecessary expenditure. There are strong views about who should be at the 'receiving end' of advertisements. For example, many parents resent the quantity of advertising for children's toys which appears during children's TV programmes. There is an assumption that all advertising is essentially dishonest. Of course, the Advertising Standards Authority (ASA) and the Independent Television Commission (ITC) exist to prevent the use of dishonest advertisements and the ASA regularly publishes bulletins detailing complaints made and the action taken. The ASA is important for media owners as well as consumers, as by monitoring advertising it helps to preserve the good reputation of the media. However, there is concern about under-representation of certain groups in society in advertising. Certainly, if advertising were taken to represent society as a whole, we might conclude that:

- only white people buy cars
- children with learning disabilities never eat
- wheelchair users never take holidays.

Too clever?

A series of advertisements for the clothing company Benetton provoked a lot of discussion and argument when it ran a few years ago. Taking as its theme 'the United

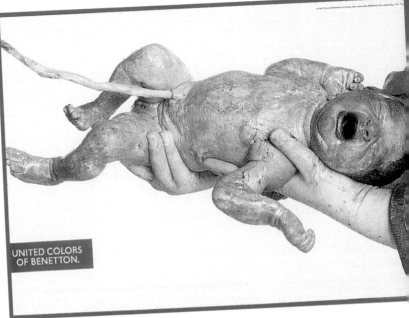

UNITED COLORS OF BENETTON.

A bad move? Is this image too strong for a clothing advertisement?

Colours of Benetton', the original implication was that the diverse cultures of the world were united in their appreciation of Benetton clothing – a rather exaggerated but essentially harmless notion which mainly used an ethnic mix of subjects to illustrate the idea. However, as the campaign progressed and developed, various other images were used – a newborn baby, an AIDS victim, the scene of an accident and so on. The implication was now even more extravagant – that Benetton clothing was somehow as fundamental to the human condition as the situations depicted in the advertisements and that, whatever ills afflicted the world, humanity remained united in its appreciation of the company's products.

Clearly, the objection was that these images were trivialized by their association with something as frivolous as clothing. This stance is borne out by the frequent depiction of other victims in different contexts, which do not attract disapproval. Government advertisements which deal with the law or which reinforce public safety are notable among these. Examples include:

• anti-drug campaigns depicting the devastating effect of heroin on a user
• seasonal campaigns against drunken driving (one of which featured home video footage of a child victim)
• fireworks safety advertisements featuring accident victims.

Gain versus benefit

The chief issue here is that of exploitation. Society has become highly sensitized to advertising as a media phenomenon, and reacts strongly to elements within it that it finds objectionable. The ASA and the ITC deal with complaints from people who object to particular advertisements.

The prospect of an advertiser making material gain through the misfortune of any individual is generally unacceptable. However, where advertising may be seen to be beneficial to the community at large, such judgements do not apply.

It's not what you've got, it's who you show it to

In addition to these specific instances, advertising must also be seen to be appropriate to the wider culture in which it is used.

Global branding and international advertising mean that it is important for advertisers and their agencies to be aware of how different cultures view advertising. For example, in Saudi Arabia, it is illegal to use photographs of women in advertisements at all, whereas in many European countries it is perfectly usual to depict topless female models in advertisements for skin care products or even other products related (sometimes tenuously) to bodily health – e.g. mineral water. The availability of different audiences via different media often has a further effect on what kind of advertising is acceptable in which media. For example, cinema advertising appearing alongside films with an 18 certificate often features adult themes. These advertisements would not be shown either alongside films for younger audiences or on television.

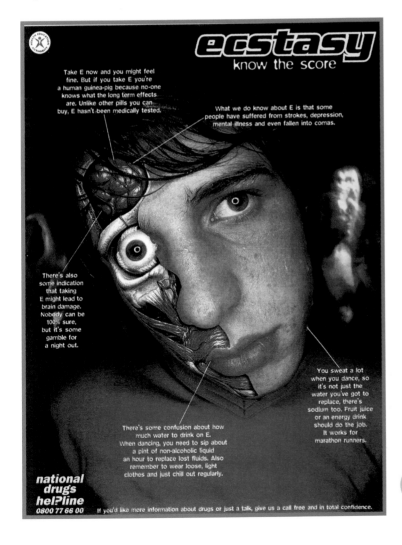

Objections to this kind of advertising are rarely raised.

Advertising as a subject

Concepts and methods taken from advertising are always cropping up in other places.

Real life?

Advertising is now so much a part of our lives that it has become a frequent subject for the media that carry it, as if its status has changed from that of being a paying visitor to that of a guest.

This cross-influencing of advertising with other forms of information – TV shows, films, fiction and so on – seems to bear out David Ogilvy's contention (see page 10) that advertising is, first and foremost, a carrier of information; and one defining characteristic of information is that it can be expressed in more than one form.

The art world has often used advertising as a subject or, indeed, as a medium. The artist David Troostwyk once used radio advertising as a medium for 'word-art'.

Back to earth ...

Of course, not all examples are as esoteric as this. The 'Gold Blend couple', whose romantic liaisons sustained a long-running TV campaign for this brand of coffee, had their adventures concluded for them in an imaginary ending which appeared in a women's magazine.

Advertising is often the theme for comedy shows and films. In *Every Home Should Have One*, a film starring the comedian Marty Feldman, the hero is an advertising executive who has to come up with ideas for advertising frozen porridge. More recently, the TV comedy series, *The Creatives*, is set in an advertising agency.

Comedians such as Jasper Carrott have constructed entire TV entertainment shows around the theme of TV advertising, often using advertising from countries other than the UK. Much of this humour relies on the fact that many kinds of advertising look very odd when seen by other cultures.

AUDIO ARTS
SUPPLEMENT

DAVID TROOSTWYK
ADVERTISEMENT OF AN IDEA 1976

On sunday february 8th 1976 an idea was advertised on a London commercial radio station, Capital Radio Ltd. This is a condensed recording of the original three hour transmission during which nine identical 15 second commercials advertised and repeated the text of an idea. This recording has retained, without alteration, approximately 45 seconds of the actual programme material that immediately preceded and immediately followed each of the nine 15 second commercials. The text of the advertisement is one of a series of texts applied to various other forms of work by the artist David Troostwyk.

This is a supplement to Audio Arts magazine
Editor: William Furlong.
AUDIO ARTS, 30 Gauden Road, London SW4 6LT

This piece of 'word-art' was first broadcast as radio advertising.

The subhead in this magazine article is a catch phrase from advertising.

... and elsewhere

Science fiction has often used advertising as a theme. One humorous story, by the British author Brian Aldiss, describes how, in the future, every house will have only two rooms. One will contain the television, which will be programmed to address you by name and ask you whether you have bought certain products. The other room stores all the things the TV advertising persuades you to buy.

Geoff Ryman, another British author, depicts advertisements as small artificial life forms which walk around promoting their designated products.

Stealth adspeak

Most interesting of all is the way in which certain examples of advertising **copy** have become part of our everyday language.

The catch-phrase 'Avon calling!' was once used by the Avon cosmetics company during an advertising campaign to promote their door-to-door selling technique. This phrase became widely known and still resurfaces from time to time. In this context (above) it is used as a headline about a rock band. Obvious, really. However, the use of the phrase offers a useful insight into the age of the writer, who is presumably old enough to remember it!

Where will it all end?

The sophistication and complexity of advertising's role in the media is likely to continue for as long as fresh thinking is available on how to unite products with markets. However, advertising is now an aspect of popular culture. Antique and period advertisement materials, from vintage Coca-Cola signs to old posters, have now become highly collectable. It seems likely that the future history of advertising will be described both in economic and cultural terms.

When the tail wags the dog!

THE POWER OF ADVERTISING – AND THE EQUALLY POWERFUL WAY THAT PEOPLE RELATE TO ADVERTISING – CAN BE SEEN IN MANY FEATURES OF EVERYDAY LIFE. SOMETIMES THE EFFECT OF ADVERTISING IS FAR-REACHING. SOMETIMES IT PRODUCES VERY SURPRISING RESULTS. HERE ARE A FEW EXAMPLES:

ADVERTISING AND MYTH THE SUPPOSEDLY TRADITIONAL IMAGE OF FATHER CHRISTMAS IS BASED ON AN ADVERTISING CONCEPT FOR COCA-COLA. ORIGINALLY DEPICTED EITHER AS A SAINT OR AN ELF, IT WASN'T UNTIL 1931 THAT THE IMAGE OF 'SANTA CLAUS' AS A JOCULAR, HUMAN-SIZED FIGURE BECAME KNOWN THROUGH THIS ADVERTISING CAMPAIGN. SANTA'S DEEP RED ROBES CONVENIENTLY MATCHED THE COLOUR USED ON COCA-COLA BOTTLES – AN IDEA REVIVED FOR ITS 1998 PRE-CHRISTMAS TV ADVERTISING CAMPAIGN. ON A SIMILAR THEME, RUDOLPH THE RED-NOSED REINDEER (IMMORTALIZED IN THE CHRISTMAS SONG) WAS CREATED IN 1939 BY AN ADVERTISING WRITER FOR THE MONTGOMERY WARD COMPANY IN THE USA.

ADVERTISING AND THE PUBLIC GOOD PERHAPS THE BEST EXAMPLES OF ADVERTISING AS AN INFORMATION SOURCE ARE 'PRODUCT RECALL' ADVERTISEMENTS. THESE OCCASIONALLY APPEAR IN THE PRESS WHEN A BATCH OF PRODUCTS, ALREADY DISTRIBUTED TO SHOPS AND SOLD TO CONSUMERS, IS SUBSEQUENTLY FOUND TO BE FAULTY – PERHAPS DANGEROUSLY SO. THE ADVERTISEMENTS USUALLY ADVISE BUYERS HOW TO OBTAIN A FREE MODIFICATION, REPLACEMENT OR REFUND. IT IS INTERESTING THAT UNDER THESE CIRCUMSTANCES, WHEN INFORMATION MUST BE CONVEYED VERY URGENTLY TO ALL POSSIBLE RECIPIENTS AS EFFICIENTLY AS POSSIBLE, ADVERTISING IS JUDGED TO BE THE MOST EFFECTIVE METHOD.

ADVERTISING AND PUBLIC DISAPPROVAL DISTRUST OF THE WHOLE IDEA OF ADVERTISING REMAINS WIDESPREAD. THE US MAGAZINE *STAY FREE!* IS DEVOTED ENTIRELY TO ATTACKING THE ADVERTISING INDUSTRY.

ADVERTISING FUNDING THE (NEW) MEDIA JUST AS THE REGIONAL PRESS WAS EVENTUALLY ABLE TO SUSTAIN FREE NEWSPAPERS FUNDED ENTIRELY BY ADVERTISING, YOU CAN NOW ACCESS THE INTERNET VIA SERVICE PROVIDERS, SUCH AS FREESERVE, WHO DON'T CHARGE A SUBSCRIPTION. HOWEVER, IN ORDER TO STAY CONNECTED, USERS MUST ACCESS THE SERVICE FOR A SPECIFIED MINIMUM PERIOD OF TIME ON A REGULAR BASIS. THIS OBVIOUSLY MAKES THE SERVICE PROVIDER MORE ATTRACTIVE TO ADVERTISERS.

ADVERTISING AND CLIENT DEMAND MCCANN ERICKSON, THE ADVERTISING AGENCY FOR COCA-COLA (THEM AGAIN!) IN THE USA, STIPULATES THAT THEIR CLIENT'S PRESS ADVERTISING SHOULD NOT APPEAR ADJACENT TO ARTICLES COVERING **HARD NEWS**, SEX, DRUGS, MEDICINE, HEALTH, 'NEGATIVE DIET INFORMATION' (E.G. ANOREXIA), FOOD, POLITICS, THE ENVIRONMENT, RELIGION OR 'ARTICLES CONTAINING VULGAR LANGUAGE', AS THESE WOULD CLASH WITH THE PRODUCT'S IMAGE. COULD THIS POTENTIALLY RESULT IN UNSCRUPULOUS PUBLISHERS ADJUSTING EDITORIAL MATERIAL TO AVOID THIS?

Glossary

advertorials advertising features in magazines which are designed to resemble editorial coverage

airtime time on radio or TV

audited checked by independent accountants

brand a distinctive name for one or more products or services (e.g. Nike)

brand loyalty an exceptional level of consumer approval of, and support for, a brand

copy text used in press advertising or as editorial content

creative relating to areas of advertising involving ideas and concepts, copywriting or scriptwriting, and design

creative team the group of people, usually at an advertising agency, who produce the ideas, visuals and texts/scripts for advertisements; often just one copywriter and one designer

corporate entertainment social events arranged by companies to enhance their image or promote products or services

cult following hyper-enthusiastic (but not necessarily widespread) support for a product or personality, often non-mainstream and tending to exclude non-supporters

demographers people who carry out demographic research

demographic relating to demographics – the study of the population by age, wealth, gender, location, etc.

digital a means of transmitting and storing information using computer-derived technology

disposable income income that is not used up in paying household expenses or other financial commitments and can therefore be spent on whatever the earner wishes

editorial sponsorship when an advertiser pays to attach their brand to an editorial feature – often presented as '… in association with …'

environment the content and appearance of the editorial matter surrounding an advertisement

hard news news covering important issues in a serious, informative way

marketing campaign a planned sequence of marketing activities to promote a product or service

marketing mix the combination of activities in a marketing campaign, which can include advertising, sales promotion, public relations and so on

market research discovering what consumers want, usually in connection with a particular type of product

market share the portion of the overall market accounted for by a particular product or service

media buying/planning buying or planning airtime, press space, etc. for advertising

media owners companies which own any medium in which advertising can be bought

online provided by computer, usually from an external source

penetration the extent to which a medium reaches its intended readership or audience

piped recorded or broadcast music relayed to many locations in a large space, such as a hotel or factory

print run the overall quantity of copies of a publication that are printed. This is not the same as the circulation, as a certain number of these copies will not be sold

product placement supplying recognizable, branded products for use in films and TV programmes

production values the amount of investment allocated to the overall quality of production. In magazine publishing, this would refer to the quality of the paper, the amount of full-colour printing and so on

profit centres departments or activities within a commercial organization which exist to make money as opposed to spending it – the latter are 'cost centres'

reader offer goods or services offered, often by mail, to the readers of a magazine or newspaper by the publisher, often in association with a manufacturer

review editorial coverage in a magazine or newspaper which assesses the quality of a product

rolling displays electrically-controlled devices (e.g. illuminated red dot-matrix displays) which display a constantly-changing message

samples small examples of products, usually provided free to potential customers in the hope that they will become regular buyers

sponsorship providing money or other kinds of support to an organization that usually has a desirable image but which needs external funding to function; the sponsor then receives a package of benefits such as appearing in the organization's publicity

storyboard a sequence of sketched or computer-generated illustrations which show how the action in a film, TV programme or commercial could proceed

teletext text-based information transmitted alongside TV broadcasts which can be viewed with a suitable TV set

tracking study an analysis of the effectiveness of an advertising or **marketing campaign** which traces the process from producer to consumer via the media; often used to evaluate the success rate of particular media and styles of advertising

trial presenting a new product to a small sector of its potential market, such as within a specific geographical region, to get an early idea of consumer reactions

wastage the element of a readership or audience that unavoidably falls outside the market for an advertised product. For example, TV ads for Intel computer chips are not relevant to non-computer-users

Index